What Child Is This?

What Child Is This?

Readings and Prayers
for Advent/Christmas

By
SAMUEL H. MILLER

Selected and Arranged by
Ernst E. Klein

FORTRESS PRESS   PHILADELPHIA

———————

Library of Congress Cataloging in Publication Data

Miller, Samuel Howard, 1900–
  What child is this?

  1. Advent — Prayer-books and devotions — English.
2. Christmas — Prayer-books and devotions — English.
I. Klein, Ernst, 1916–   II. Title.
BV40.M54   242 '.33   82–5084
ISBN 0–8006–1638–3   AACR2

———————

9588B82 Printed in the United States of America 1–1638

Contents

Introduction — An Authentic Pastoral Ministry

Samuel Howard Miller was minister of the Old Cambridge Baptist Church from 1934 to 1959. In 1959 he became Dean of Harvard Divinity School until his death in 1968, only a few months before retirement.

Those who know his first book, *The Life of the Soul,* and his *Prayers for Daily Use* (now unfortunately out of print), know Dean Miller's unerring insights into the Christian faith and the human condition, expressed in language characterized by vivid and powerful imagery drawn from daily life, as well as by lofty flights of poetic imagination.

"Sam" Miller was not a saint in the usual sense. He knew the right names for things and people involved in the monstrous evils of depression and war, as well as the ordinary indignities of daily existence. In conversation, his language could be as forthright and salty as a seaman's. He often spoke of his own "embarrassments" before the Lord, and in his prayers assumed that others shared this experience, which made some nice people quite uncomfortable!

He did not believe in labels such as "liberal/

evangelical" or "fundamentalist/modernist," seeking to be nothing more than a humble follower of Jesus Christ and "an honest man of God."

Like every Christian, Sam Miller's heart was full of hope. But his world view begins with a tragic sense of life. As a boy he lost a brother to death; as a father he lost two sons in World War II. Through the years, he learned not to expect too much from life. . . . The naive optimism of some advocates of the so-called social gospel was an abomination. The notion that good intentions and good will, with intelligent planning and progress in technology, could produce a society essentially free from evil and suffering, he called "a temptation of the devil." The kingdom comes, according to Miller, not where people rush about in frantic activism—from whatever good motives—but rather where people fall on their knees and quiet their souls to hear the angels sing. Right conduct and true community begin to happen on a small scale, as people live out their thankfulness for new revelations of God's grace and joy.

For twenty-four years the plain people of the

Old Cambridge Baptist Church, including a few professors and some students from Harvard and M.I.T., entrusted the care of their souls to this earnest young man of God. Sometimes they did not understand his preaching. Always, they understood his prayers. They knew beyond all doubt that the Rev. Samuel H. Miller was lifting their souls, with all the stains and ambiguities of this wicked world, up to God for cleansing, for blessing, for courage, and for joy.

His generous ecumenical spirit found full expression as he led the many-faceted faculty at Harvard. The Catholic-Protestant Colloquium with Cardinal Bea was a milestone on the way to Christian unity. He was a warm friend of the late Cardinal Richard Cushing of Boston. Sam Miller's heart was simply too big to be confined to one sect, one tradition, or one people. He knew the largeness of God's mercy. . . .

Miller's theology is difficult to characterize, impossible to label. He received the standard liberal theological education at Colgate University (after giving up his first impulse to become an engineer at M.I.T.). Yet he was not a liberal. He was one of the first in this country to immerse himself in the writings of Kierkegaard, yet he was much more than an existentialist. Some of his insights anticipate Paul Tillich, that is, the "dimension of depth" and the correlation between culture and Christianity. Accepting the results of the critical study of the Scriptures, Miller insisted that the religious experiences recorded there are still available to people today, to which his own life is eloquent testimony! He found new meanings in the ancient doctrines of classical Christianity, especially in the Creation, the Incarnation, and the Resurrection. He was an irenic Christian, a man for all ages! This is why these prayers and thoughts on Advent/Christmas are so fresh and timely for our day!

This new collection of prayers and thoughts for Advent/Christmas is sent forth in the hope that many who have known Samuel H. Miller will have new occasions to rejoice and participate anew in his authentic ministry, and that others also may come under the influence of this saintly and honest man of God. They are not intended to be fed wholesale to a congregation or to substitute for the minister's own quest and spiritual discipline; rather, it is hoped they will aid both pastor and people in discovering ever-new Epiphanies, and in celebrating the ever-recurring miracle of the Incarnation.

Cambridge, Mass.   ERNST E. KLEIN
February 1979

A Lovely Mystery

Today is the first day of December, and, whether we will it or not, a warmth will begin to creep across the earth from that timeless manger where the Eternal was born so young and lovely. Were all other mysteries evaded, this mystery would still persist — how a little child born to humble parents, cradled in a beast's manger, should send across the tumultuous plains of time such a gracious climate of innocent-hearted love to us of a foreign race and a different day. In the very midst of winter, it will be a springtime for the hearts of the world, our iron earth of unyielding sternness will thaw, and the green shoots of new mercy will flaunt their beauty against the cold but dying winds of our wintry suspicion, and all of us, old and young, will find a homier world, more forgiving and like to God, than we have often known but lost through care and fear.

God and Father of us all, in whom our joy finds perfect peace, enter, we beseech thee, into the crowded inn of our life, quiet the tumult and the disorder, and let thy strength impel us to make an ample place for the advent of thy Son, our Lord, Jesus Christ. Move us by such joy as we have had in Jesus Christ and in thee to praise thy holy will and wisdom. Make us glad, after the way of thy spirit, through Jesus Christ. Amen.

12- 19-99

Christmastide of Joy

The stars are easily forgotten in the cities. Unseen, obliterated by blazing lights and high buildings, they swing their splendored arch silently across the heavens. Yet they belong to the human scene. They lend to it a sense of cosmic perspective. Though we dwell on a tiny earth, we are companions of the stars, caught in the same vast web of creation. This is indeed no picayune destiny, except we make it so.

And now the Christmastide of joy rises to its full, and the story is told again of how the humblest of mortals, the Son of man, was born with a star standing over the manger where he lay. Read the story as you may, make of it what you will, but do not miss the daring implication that the farthest reaches of the universe wait upon the humblest occurrences of this world. There is a star over you, and over all whom you know. There are eternal implications in the scenes of earth; do not miss them — they are for the guidance of the wise. This life is a web of beauty and strength, holding the stars and little children together in a mighty purpose, larger than our understanding.

Father of all Souls, we give thee thanks for Jesus Christ through whom thou did unmistakably disclose thy love to men. In his presence, we know how much we have given ourselves to shadows of unreality, killing time and distracting life, exhausting our souls and smothering our freedom, until the glory wherewith life was created passed from us and left us only a hollow dream, a vain burden. Let his spirit enter us to awaken our neglected depths, to stir us mightily by sight and shock of eternal things, and to guide us into paths of faith and simplicity that we might be servants of thy glory in all our works, through Jesus Christ our Lord. Amen.

Astounded by the Impossible

"instead of the thorn shall come up the fir tree"

For a long time we have been intent on the law-abiding regularity of our world. On it we have erected the tremendous edifices of science and engineering, and through it we have presumed the dependableness of God.

The gains of such work are obvious. A great deal of what seemed to be unpredictable caprice has now been drawn within the pattern of definite prediction. Yet one must say, in life as we humans know it, there is considerable surprise. Things

happen unexpectedly. The web of circumstance and experience is so complex, perhaps the power of God is so resourceful and creative, that at any time we may be astounded by the "impossible." Certainly there is no other way to describe the amazing events of the first Christmas. Surely there is no one so soul-dead he cannot recall in his own lifetime the sudden "turn" of events, the unexpected of which there was no premonition, occurring with unbelievable abruptness. One does not stretch the truth to say that God does do the most unexpected things.

Bend Low, O my God, from thy heights of holiness and from the heart's center of full giving, and look mercifully upon us who, dwelling amid the insecurities of this mortal life, are tempted to guard every advantage and keep everything as if our life could be guaranteed by what we have or what we enjoy. Help us to discover again that bread broken with one in need is bread shared with thee. Make our hearts open handed, and if it imperils the petty securities of habit and place, let it be to the saving of our souls in Christ's name. Amen.

We Need Christmas

How shall the heart, bearing its burden of loneliness and shame and grief, sing the songs of Christmas gladness? The truth is, we need Christmas. We need it so deeply, so desperately, that we will celebrate it though our hearts wear sackcloth and ashes. We will celebrate "something" in it that the world and all its fury cannot dim or obliterate. We will keep it as a "sign," a sign that we believe in a world of "peace on earth, good will to men," though all the appearances are against it and earth itself seems to have been turned into something more like hell. Fundamentally and ultimately, we believe that God will not forsake us, even at our worst. We have hope — a star over the new born child!

Oh God, in the fog and fury of this dark age, keep the inner world of heart and mind in us clear and strong, that we may not be buffeted from our course by the wild winds of chaos and seas of bitterness. Help us onward through all kinds of weather to follow patiently the north star of thine eternal purpose and, if darkness and chaos hide it, hold us firm by every remembrance and hope to do thy will through Jesus Christ our Lord. Amen.

12-21-86 PM

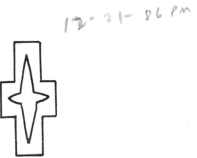

If Christmas Could Only Last

"Mary kept all these things and pondered them in her heart."

There are some days in the year which seem like ladders, by which we climb to a purer air and a much broader view of life. Christmas is certainly such a day. Yet how quickly and imperceptibly we drop back to the old level, with only a haunting dream by which we remember the mirth and mystery of our vision. But what if we could establish ourselves on that higher level, to live with a greater magnitude of sight and power. If, in other words, Christmas could only last — the wonder of it, the simplicity of it, the thoughtfulness of the wise and the adoration of the humble, if fears could be cast out and faith could move in — permanently!

Well, that is exactly what Christianity purports to be — a perennial celebration of joy and peace, such as some enjoy only at Christmas time.

Mighty and merciful God, born into this flesh, and in this flesh living in this world, we seek the support and refuge of every earthly thing and power, and though life brutally and forcibly forces us to drop one thing after another, we return again and again to put our trust in things obvious to sense and use, although there is no hope but in thee and no lasting joy save in thy kingdom. Lead us, therefore, beyond all the outer ramparts of this changing earth to the eternal city of thy grace through Jesus Christ our Lord, that we may give thanks unto thee forever and forever. Amen.

Recognizing Christ Who Comes

"the Jews had already agreed that if any man confessed to be the Christ, they would excommunicate him"

"He came to his own — to people who had been praying for His coming, who had been waiting, and hoping, and counting on it, and then he was not recognized. "They knew him not." They judged him to be a blasphemer, a wine-bibber, an upsetter of people's opinion, one whom they thought wise to put to death.

Strange story this! A nation, over many centuries, longing for something and yet refusing it when it came! At our safe distance, it seems so plain that they refused to accept Jesus because they were not strong enough to really want their prayers to come true. They would have had to revolutionize their way of living.

This is the Advent season! May we ask how true it is that our prayers for Christ's coming, for the realization of God's kingdom on earth is merely a dream we refuse to seriously put into practice.

Eternal God of mercy, if weariness of body, or confusion of mind, or anxiety of heart, compels our lips to keep silent, or our souls to remain in the shadow of uncertainty, then by thy mighty love, lift up our eyes to see Jesus Christ, a man of sorrows, but with such strength of faith as to bring joy to joyless men and freedom to those who had lost all hope. Grant us knowledge of how, having come from thee, he laid thy benediction on all imperfect things of earth, and led men's souls, long lost, back to their Maker, the Lord of all Life. Teach us by the swift glory of his spirit how to live abundantly in faith, joyously, and with kindness. Whatsoever joys are ours, whatsoever dreams fulfilled and deeds accomplished, let them utter their song in perfect delight and without restraint, through Jesus Christ, our Lord. Amen.

Higher Levels of Goodness

"except your righteousness exceed the right-eousness . . ."

There are all kinds of goodness in the world, all grades and levels, from the kind that seems more malicious and hard-hearted than evil to the kind that seems to be unearthly wise and, in its wisdom, very kind. The great difficulty is to get from one level to another and better one.

And the essence of the difficulty seems to be that goodness at any level produces a kind of satisfaction, a "now I have arrived" feeling, as though this is all that could possibly be required. It is as if goodness congeals very quickly, and, once congealed, it is hard to change. Yet surely nothing is more evident than that an arrested development in goodness is as obnoxious and death-dealing as anywhere else in life. Let us get on with our living, with the fulfillment of the stages that lead up to the higher levels of goodness.

In the world it is still true, as in Christ's time, that the good man may be the one to resist the

revelations and messengers of God's new truth. Nicodemus was a good man, but that was not enough. He needed to be born again to perceive the new world of Christ's kingdom.

O God most high, most near, open the deep places of our hearts, so that our joy may not be selfishly shallow in this hour of Christ's coming, but with knowledge of this world's sorrow, uplifted and transformed by the timeless grace of his spirit. Deliver us from all quibbling unbelief, and set us free by the swift flight of our soul's aspirations to enter into Christmas as men humbled to a joy greater than they expected or earned. Wherever there are children, may gifts be holy in the name of Christ the Child. Amen.

(12 - 24 - 85.)

The Right Track

"What do you want?"

The chief end of man, it was once said, was to glorify God and to enjoy him forever. Our ways of living and thinking have changed enough now so that saying has something strange about it, a bit medieval, and needs to be explained before we are sure we know what it means. Other things have moved into the center of the stage, and our attention and energy are expended in a different direction. We are not "other-worldly"; we believe in one world at a time, in doing things, going places, getting somewhere. We no longer divide humankind into saints and sinners, but characteristically into successes and failures. We explain history in terms of progress, and personal life in terms of getting ahead in the world. We are very practical people.

But—I can hear another voice saying, "What shall it profit a man . . . ?" I find myself asking, What is life for? These days and nights, the labor of it and all its perplexities and pains, the anguish of growing, the embarrassment of error, and the

shame of sin, all the innumerable burdens and revelations of experience — all for what? What is the appropriate profit, the adequate gain? When I've finished however many years of living I may be given, I should like to think I had been on the right track however slowly I had traveled, and not in a blind alley.

O God, now with one year almost gone and another in prospect, we stand before thee in the long panorama of the world's history, humbled beyond any expression of our humility. Our days are brief, our sight is small, our ways are fraught with great mystery. Be merciful and strengthen our minds and hearts to endure our destiny in such a world as this, and by the grace of thy will impel us to give witness to the bright, indomitable flame of thy Spirit's kingdom amid all earth's darkness. Amen.

Endless Wonder

Most of us are afraid of the mysteries. Dark, imponderable, threatening, they seem to be the source of all our trouble and tragedy. We assault them with blind fury, ransack them with relentless greed for whatever facts we can find, or deny them with an ill-disguised pose of cynical indifference. Mystery has all the reputation of being our enemy, and so we retaliate as best we can, by frantic attacks or evasive cunning.

But to love the mysteries — strange as it appears, and as impossible to most moderns — is the act of faith. To suspend willingly our disbelief, to drop our omnipotent air of critical judgment, to recover a certain innocence, known to us as children, and not at all unlike a wiser kind of wisdom than any we have known since such days of wonder, is to enter into a world where heavenly anthems are still sung over the troubled earth and the humblest of men find a way to serve the Eternal Lord. The mysteries are black with despair, until faith follows the Star of God and finds not knowledge but endless wonder, in the presence of the Radiant Word made flesh.

Dear God, Father of all mercy, by whose forgiveness our joy is made free, grant us also that joy by which all grievances, all remembered misunderstandings, and all the blinding half-sights of other days are forgotten, that we may dwell together in peace and in gladness.

We enter at this season by thy grace into a joy we did not create, and into a mystery we cannot fathom. Generation after generation we have been blessed by the Babe of Bethlehem, and in him we have seen the very ways of thy perfect will and infinite wisdom. Make us what thou wilt, deliver us from the prides and conceits of worldly wisdom, recover the impulses of childlikeness in all of us, and let the roots of our life grow deep in the spirit of these holy days, in which we celebrate the incarnation of the holy word in the flesh of the Son of man. Amen.

No Other Day Like It

This is Christmas Day! There is not another day like it in all the year. It is as if we had been climbing for the last month with our eyes on this one goal! Now that we are here — a little spent for our struggle perhaps — we are enjoying the occasion to the fullest! No small achievement this! We have reached a high summit in human relationships, a summit of good will, of joyous friendship, of thoughtful generosity. We may slip back to a harder, blinder world, but for today we are living in joy — where we were meant to live.

O God, we acknowledge before thee, from whom nothing is hid, that this is no casual hour, though we have often treated it so. Before the beauty of thy holiness we present ourselves, our minds crisscrossed with idle distractions, our hearts smudged with the dirt and stain of this world's shabbiness, our souls not yet grown to strength and wisdom, hobbled by doubts and half-hearted hopes. Stand us on our feet, O God, and lift up our eyes to see thy kingdom in all its humble, saving glory, that we may be delivered from our spiritual invalidism and take our place among the marching saints and pilgrims who seek the greater light. Amen.

Seeing God's Labor in the Earth

"Blessed is the man who takes delight in the law of the Eternal"

"To take delight in the law of the Eternal!" How much more common it is that men give to the Bible an easy but sterile reference in which there is neither light nor joy, and which leads sooner or later to a complete neglect, not only of the Bible, but of God and the realm of things eternal.

"Delight in the law of the Lord!" The Bible is full of men whose passionate pursuit of things spiritual, of truth that would last, of realities that were permanent, their earnestness, genius of insight, and patient zeal of imagination match well the remarkable efforts of the men of science of our own time who have been exploring the dark mysteries of nature. These earlier "scientists," interested in the knowledge of God, deserve a better understanding than the kind of sterile respect which elevates them beyond and out of our present human situation.

Father, we have grown so frenzied in our activities that we no longer see thy labor in the earth, but, intent upon our own work, grow blind to thine. We have changed so many things that we are not conscious of the unchanging. We are building up and tearing down, anxious only for the advantage of the hour. Our striving has earned so much, that we cannot believe thy best gifts are free. We beseech thee, therefore, O God, to manifest thyself anew, that our souls may once again be revived by sight of Thee and by sure knowledge of thy glory. Amen.

An Exceptional Day

"just as it was in the days of Lot — eating, drinking, buying, selling, planting, building — "

How the days, flowing swiftly, carry the years with them. Day after day, the routine grows deeper, the paths we tread become ruts, and the tasks we do can be done automatically, without anxiety or enthusiasm. Thus the common run of days looks dull, flat, and quite unexciting. Life grows casual, and, like blinded Samson, his glory lost, walks endless circles hopelessly, waiting for the exceptional to happen.

What is it that makes a day exceptional, lifts it out of the common run, exalts it to a high and significant level in man's imagination? Somehow its glory was revealed, its meaning manifested, its internal significance made plain. Someone saw its exceptional character underneath its unpretentious appearance. Some days are made by catastrophes, it is true, but others are made by insight.

People say that nothing ever happens to them; what they ought to say is that they see nothing in

what is happening — that would be truer. Events are nothing at all, until there is sight to see the miracle in them. The common run of days is merely that portion of time we have not redeemed for eternity by our creative imagination.

Eternal One, thou who art the Lord of all our striving, and the strength with which we search, bring us near unto thy glory, that we may worship, not in the dullness of habit too often repeated, but with such fresh sight of thy spirit's beauty and wondrous mercy, that our hearts shall leap with joy and our whole life respond to the mighty urgency of thy power. For this hour, at least, deliver us from halting doubts and confusions; thrust us by the wonder of thy greatness beyond the limits of our caution and care, through Jesus Christ our Lord. Amen.

Beyond the Hills

"he looked for a city, which hath foundations, whose maker and builder is God"

What lies beyond the hills . . . ? Restless hearts, pilgrim feet — these cannot be restrained from finding out. Whatever is beyond the hills tingles in the air and, like a far off trumpet call, hangs in the bright silence of the sky, easily heard despite the noise of trade and the shouts of busy men. Once heard, the ear cannot forget, the eyes will look beyond the things they see, and the soul will stand and wait on tireless tip-toe for the first word of faith. For such men, the ruts and routines of what has already been established cannot be home. Their spirits are marked with the sign of Him who created the earth out of nothing, and the power of that image will give them strength to forfeit everything for the new life.

Beyond the hills — beyond this rim of habit, this solid circle of established repetition, this rampart that hems us in and makes us safe, is there a land waiting to be "opened up"? Or is the bulwark so high or so mighty that we shall not hear the silver

spears of trumpets shattering the sky, or that hearing we shall not have the courage to go despite uncertainty and peril? Unless a man loses his life, shall he find it?

Almighty God, grant to all homeless children the grace of our Lord Jesus, who found shelter with the beasts of the field when there was no room at the inn; let him who had no place to lay his head abide with the refugees in the bitter trials of their flight and exile. For all who carry the cross of this world's sin and violence, reveal the vision that gave him power to endure the shame for the joy that was set before him. Wherever a cup of cold water is given in mercy's name so that life is shared, disclose the glory of him in whom all thirst is quenched; and bring to all men whose dreams are still of thee and of thy way despite the darkness and cruelty of our time the strength and faith to persevere until thy kingdom come, and thy will be done. Amen.

Worship That Disturbs

"Woe is me! for mine eyes have seen the Lord of hosts"

If this is worship, if it is a deliberate attempt to invade the Eternal, to come face to face with Almighty God, to strip ourselves of every deceit and illusion, to plead with the Lord of Creation to work his will through us and bring us to newness of life, to reach up out of our infinite darkness and mystery for some light and leading — if this is worship, and not a mild concealment or a languid fantasy of habit, we may be probed so deeply by the finger of God and be forced to act so violently that we may leave this hour spiritually spent and sore. Then if we value our comfort, that is, our spiritual stagnation or somnolence more than our salvation, we may never return, choosing to find some pleasanter church where men go through the motions of a religious act, but never wake the ailing soul, drifting back to nothing through the dreamy haze of an undisturbed coma. This is the house of God, not an anesthesia chamber.

O God, we have spread smooth words over the deep mysteries, turned our eyes from the terror of the soul, and lost ourselves in minor distractions. We have made our worship a hollow sepulchre, whited with the appearance of reverent phrases but inwardly dead. We praise thee with subtle evasions and cunning care, for we know that thou are a consuming fire before which our lives could not stand in peace. Come, show us where we stand, what we have been doing, how we have side stepped thee, and propped up our pride with a vain righteousness! Save us through Jesus Christ our Lord. Amen.

God's Mighty Plan

"That those things which cannot be shaken may remain"

It is a trite and inadequate saying that the world in which we live is changing. Violence has upset it, confusion and bewilderment possess it, and all kinds of ideas and plans are afoot for the future. Things we thought solid have turned out to be mere shadows, and some very shadowy things, by our previous reckoning, have come to stand the strain and pressure of our desperate souls.

Darkness does not change the stars. Storm and cloud may obscure them or hide them, but they remain. So this world's vast storm may "black out" many things for a time, but the "foolishness of God," the grace of Jesus, the glad news of the gospel — all the seemingly impractical, unreal intangibles of the spirit will reappear and manifest their eternal character and enduring worth. It is Christian wisdom to keep in mind these things when the storm is at its worst, and they seem to be overwhelmed by stronger and more powerful forces.

Our God, to whom we turn
When weary with illusion
Whose stars serenely burn
Above this earth's confusion,
Thine is the mighty plan,
The steadfast order sure,
in which the world began,
Endures and shall endure.

Serving Means Waiting

Have you ever been aggravated and exhausted by a well-intentioned bustling person who wants to do a lot for you? They rush about, work themselves into a fever, turn everything topsy-turvy to serve you — while you would be glad enough to take things as they are and have a chance to call your soul your own. Then you know how Jesus felt at Bethany — Martha was bustling!

Now some people, out of the best of intentions, "bustle about," serving God. They are furiously strenuous; they make a great clatter; they want everybody to rush about like themselves; they are in a perfect dither; and they are happy when they get the world in one. They mistake noise and motion for life.

We are not servants of a day but of eternity, not of the world but of God, not of frenzy but of creation. To serve means also to "wait."

Lord, the inn of life each of us keeps is confused by many anxieties and its joy smothered by unseeing haste. Better to keep a humbler place, with room and shelter for the nameless Word become flesh, for innocence which has no reputation, and for peace known only by the angels above and lonely shepherds watching in quiet fields. Prepare our hearts for Christmas, and if we can become like little children, with eyes for the stars and ears for heavenly anthems, grant us such joy through the grace of our Redeemer, born of Mary in Bethlehem. Amen.

Each Day Has a Right of Its Own

"sufficient unto the day"

The shadow of the future has grown to tremendous dimensions and burdens the fearful heart of the world immeasurably. Everyone is guessing what tomorrow may bring forth; everyone is preparing against its possible dangers; everyone is haunted by its unpredictableness. For a long time the world "ate, drank, and was merry," forgetting the future, but now the future has come back to lay a heavy weight on the passing hours, and we

are in danger of forgetting what there is in any day for our peace and joy.

This is not blindness but balance. It is knowing that the future has its rights, but no right to obliterate entirely the worth and reality of the present. This day, or any day, has a right of its own, a strength and a beauty, which no other day may ruin or deny. In one sense of the word, the kingdom of God, the realm of the Eternal, depends on our seeing what belongs to each day in its own inalienable right, and to affirm it and celebrate it by our joy. This, after all, is our hope for Christmas.

O God, our lives are not all alike — yet we pray together. We have lived, and living we have felt the wavering of our spirit like a flame, a flame buffeted by the wild winds of the world. We have pondered the puzzle of our existence and that deep abyss of mystery in which we live. We have known the struggle to fulfill some dim and distant destiny by deeds of common mortal effort. Now we beseech thee, by the pain of our heart's striving and by the hope of its joy as well, to grant us the grace of sight and strength to understand what thou has called us to do, that we may be faithful even unto life eternal. Amen.

Time is Now

"Are there not twelve hours in the day?"

Again the poignant drama of passing time is dramatized by the calendar sign of a new year. We know, as the poet has said, that "years are not life . . . but the shells of life," yet on such an occasion as this our hearts tremble as we see from such a vantage point the deep gulf of the year gone and the twisting, untrod road of the year coming. There is no retreat, no refuge, no shelter — just the inevitable road ahead to be walked in faith or in fear, or perhaps in ill-disguised indifference. Our bodies and our thoughts are woven of the threads of time: our days and nights are marks of her mastery; our deeds and desires are her children. Here as elsewhere in life we may lose our souls, from too much love of what is gone and too much fear or attention paid to what is not yet come. For time is now! The past is present, and all the future we shall ever know is present. The narrow alley in which we live may seem uncomfortably small and precarious, but it is also impenetrably deep and precious.

Father of all souls born into time, grant us quietness of heart while we remember, and in our remembering, give us eyes to see the work of thy spirit. We have lived and labored, each in our own way to do thy will. We have seen the slender thread on which life depends. We have been conscious of the iron tissue of time enfolding all things and ourselves, and yet we have seen time split open by the splendor of things eternal. Help us in our remembering, therefore, O God, to be strong in hope through Jesus Christ our Lord. Amen.

The Last Day of the Year

"We spend our years as a tale that is told"

This day is the last day of a year. In a way it is not different from any other we have known—the sun rising, our eyes opening, then hunger and thinking; the hours fill with words and acts falling into their little patterns or struggling to be free of them until the sun sets, the eyes grow heavy, and we lie down to that sweet oblivion of sleep. And yet it is not the same as other days, because *we* are not the same. We know it to be the last day, and in the eyes that are lifted up to glance across the swift passage of a whole year, there is a wordless mystery! A year of time, quick flowing, running through our fingers silently and forever! The days pass, one after another, inexorably, and no clutching will keep them. Yet they leave their marks upon us, upon our hands and faces, upon the spirit most of all, and our heart is filled with their

voices, laughing and weeping. A year—and life! What are these things? What have we done with them? Or what has been done to us? What is the meaning of it all and its end?

12-31-89

Dear God, what canst thou make of this year? All the living of it, the trifles and the tragedies that compound our days; all the torment of heart and struggle of the brain; all the humble labor of the body and the lonely vigil of the soul; all the fears, the confusion and the bitterness; all the hopes, the hours of peace, and the great gift of faith — what shall these add up to in thy final judgment? Be patient, O God, and guide us to walk in the way of life that we may do thy will, through Jesus Christ, our Lord. Amen.

Starting Anew

We who are conscious of the newness of this day turn to thee who art Eternal, lest in the rushing tide of time we forget the unfathomable immortality of thy Spirit. We know with shame, thou didst stand beneath the gateway of many a moment in the year past waiting for the seeing eye, while we so blindly and carelessly dallied, killing time, not knowing that eternal life was within reach. We confess that we are not strong enough of spirit to move unhampered into every new occasion with trustful freedom or quick enough of insight and understanding to love every hour that rises from the white harvest of thy sowing. But move us mightily, if or when thou dost trouble the pool of our Bethesda, to plunge out of all our habit into breath-giving life. Amen.